Seasons of Love

Woodland Poems of God's Love

May you walk in God's woods forever!

Lisa Belknap

Lisa Belknap

Veery Glade Publishing

Veery Glade Publishing
Cortland, New York 13045

For Matthew, Malin and Ezra

May you walk in God's woods forever.

Contents

For I am persuaded, that neither death,
nor life, nor angels, nor principalities, nor powers,
nor things present, nor things to come, nor height,
nor depth, nor any other creature, shall be able to
separate us from the love of God,
which is in Christ Jesus our Lord.
Romans 8:38-39

Seasons of Love

Greener than grass, sweeter than pink,
God meant the stars He made in a blink.
He'll pick daffodils
on spring's lively hills
and fill my gold tin to the brink.

Truer than blue, warmer than sun,
God meant the life He gives in His Son.
He'll lead without fail
along summer's trail
and hurry my feet to a run.

Brighter than orange, richer than brown,
God meant the joy He vows to His own.
He'll catch golden leaves
from autumn's bright trees
and make a bouquet for my crown.

Whiter than snow, bolder than red,
God meant the words He truthfully said.
He'll call a warm beam
by winter's cold stream
and melt the snowflakes on my head.

Spring

If we confess our sins,
he is faithful and just to forgive us our sins,
and to cleanse us from all unrighteousness.
1 John 1:9

The Waterfall

Down in the gorge of mist and cold
pours out a gushing, strong and bold,
that makes the hemlocks surge up tall—
the power of the waterfall.

The water dances as it sings,
and off the trees, its echo rings
to fill the woodland concert hall—
the music of the waterfall.

The flow that washes like a sea
removes the mud and creek debris,
and smoothes the jagged, rocky wall—
the cleansing of the waterfall.

The LORD of Heaven gives the might,
with mercies pouring day and night,
to send my wrongs cascading all—
the beauty of God's waterfall.

He was despised and rejected of men;
a man of sorrows, and acquainted with grief:
and we hid as it were our faces from him;
he was despised, and we esteemed him not.
Isaiah 53:3

From A Pure Stand

Jesus, the Christ, suffered,
like what falls from a pure stand,
with all majesty stripped and beauty no more,
bearing sin and hurts and a whipping strand—
the punishment humbly He bore.

Jesus, God's Son, perished,
like what dies low on the ground,
left to waste and decay, where graves take back,
cast away and disowned but not making a sound—
obedience, none did He lack.

Jesus, our Lord, descended,
like what goes under the floor,
where there is no esteem in the lengthening of day,
smitten and stricken, where shadows grow more—
the price He did willingly pay.

The Pond by the Wood

I hiked to the pond early Friday morn
through rain and mist and woods forlorn,
for the winter had torn limbs here and there,
and a heaviness clung to the morning air.

I stood on the bank by the meadow bleak
with my head hung low, down and weak,
for what have I done to deserve great love
from such a Savior and King above?

Circles spun on the water's face
when raindrops fell softly to their place,
and clouds swirled free in the pool's dark depths
when winds encircled off Heaven's steps.

Then there on the water, the sun came shining!
His words of love to me reminding;
pledging gladness through oaks as the sky turned blue
and encouraging wonder in all things new!

What grace shines upon the pond by the wood!
What joy restored and understood!
For I know Jesus loves me with all His heart,
and from me, it never, nor ever, will part.

To appoint unto them that mourn in Zion,
to give unto them beauty for ashes,
the oil of joy for mourning,
the garment of praise for the spirit of heaviness;
that they might be called trees of righteousness,
the planting of the LORD, that he might be glorified.
Isaiah 61:3

15

The Daffodil's Trumpet

For My Father

The daffodil stands by the edge of the wood
'neath a slumbering red maple tree,
and he picks up his trumpet of finest pure gold
to announce the beginning of spring.

He's early to wake from the long, bitter cold
and his yellow suit coat is a joy
which can heal the long worn out expressions of old,
and soothe the dark ages of yore.

He stands on a knoll that will carry the tune,
where the sun shines a-warm on the dew.
And he plays out a "Toot, Ala Toot-ti-ly Toot!
Wake up, trees and critters, all living things, you!"

His song wakens others and soon there are many
to proclaim the renewal of life.
Their horns call brightly! The woods, they are waking—
away with worries and strife!

The daffodil smiles in the light of our Lord
and declares our dependence on Him,
and reminds us of joy that only Christ gives
and life coming only from Him.

Lift up your heads, O ye gates;
and be ye lift up, ye everlasting doors;
and the King of glory shall come in.
Psalm 24:7

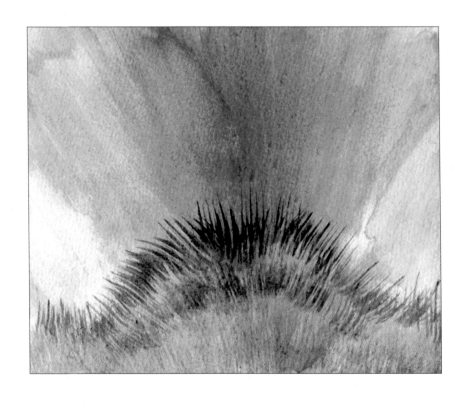

Wherefore God also hath highly exalted him,
and given him a name which is above every name:
That at the name of Jesus every knee should bow,
of things in heaven, and things in earth,
and things under the earth;
And that every tongue should confess
that Jesus Christ is Lord,
to the glory of God the Father.
Philippians 2:9-11

Victory Hill

I shout "Victory!" on the highest hill.
I shout "Joy!" where the valleys fill.
Jesus is no longer dead!

I cry "Savior!" to the meadow's end.
I cry "Friend!" where the willows bend.
Jesus fulfilled what was said!

I yell "Freedom!" to the birch trees far.
I yell "Hope!" to the furthest star.
Jesus was raised from the dead!

I speak "Mercy!" to the babbling brook.
I speak "Life!" to the woodland nook.
Jesus has done all he said!

And then, I will kneel where the grass is deep
and give to the Lord my soul to keep.
Jesus is no longer dead.

As the Father hath loved me, so have I loved you:
continue ye in my love.
John 15:9

What the Brook Sings
A Spring Sonnet

Shall I compare you to a singing brook?
You are more favored and more exquisite.
Spring waters rip the banks I overlook
and summer heat can lessen jolly wit.
Sometimes, rough singing turns to babbling quick
and ripples skip a beat in hurriedness.
Or, quality has ended by a stick
where pools have gathered foam in quietness.
But your endearing voice will resonate
and not be muddled by Earth's season's tolls.
A song together we will celebrate
of joy brought forth by Heaven's happy souls.
So long as you hear what the brook sings of.
So long as you know it is My true love.

And ye shall know the truth,
and the truth shall make you free.
John 8:32

Truth is Like a Trillium
For Malin

Truth is like a trillium
that blossoms in the spring.
It dances with the waking trees
and stirs the birds to sing.

Through winter, it lays dormant,
beneath the snowy ground.
Then with the warmth of springtime,
it stretches roots around.

It grows within the sunshine,
first budding after years.
The plant designed by Trinity
takes time to match its peers.

And there it stands a-shining,
a pure, revealing face!
The woodland floor, once bumpy bare,
now shimmers full of grace!

Truth is like a trillium.
O may my faith grow strong!
For with it, I am known and free
to bloom forever long.

24

Summer

And Mary said, My soul doth magnify the Lord,
and my spirit hath rejoiced in God my Saviour.
Luke 1:46-47

Woodland Song

Joyfully, joyfully, feathered friends call,
the chickadees and grosbeaks and orioles all,
to sing a lyric melody at opening of day,
to start the winging choir, a-chirping all the way!

Over high, over there, beside the babbling brook,
the cardinals and veeries resound in every nook;
the drumming of the ruffed grouse, the cooing of the dove,
the tapping of the woodpecker that echoes high above!

"Yahweh God! Yahweh God!", into the evening night,
hummingbirds and nuthatches turn in from their flight.
And in the final light of day, the robin sings her song.
What joy to hear the woodland birds sing praises all day long!

Where the Leaves Dance

For My Mother

A soft breeze, a gentle sigh,
I'll be where the leaves dance.
I'll look up through at skies of blue
and fall within a trance.

In relaxed state, I'll contemplate
and hear the wood thrush echoing.
His gorgeous tune releases me,
a distant place is beckoning.

How could God make these woods so fine?
All worries are asunder.
I'll close my eyes and take it in,
this quiet place of wonder.

Peace I leave with you,
my peace I give unto you:
not as the world giveth, give I unto you.
Let not your heart be troubled,
neither let it be afraid.
John 14:27

Fear none of those things which thou shalt suffer:
behold, the devil shall cast some of you into prison,
that ye may be tried; and ye shall have tribulation
ten days: be thou faithful unto death,
and I will give thee a crown of life.
Revelation 2:10

The Faithful Trail

On the faithful trail, I'll go,
where ferns are thick and greening,
and the undergrowth goes up and down,
and the trees are sometimes leaning.

But on the trail, I'll follow,
as I pass beneath basswoods,
as I walk along the touch-me-nots
and a patch of tangled dogwoods.

I'll trust when at the gully,
where the woods are dark and deepest,
and I'll cross along the cherry tree,
where the bank is all the steepest.

At trail's end, I'll have rest
in a special, hidden clearing—
in the grass, I'll watch the passing clouds,
and the warblers I'll be hearing.

Peaceful Rock

I headed for a place I know,
not wanting any clock,
where my burdened ears can hear the flow,
resting well on Peaceful Rock.

By the brook, I'll sit and close my eyes,
where the canopy is thick,
and contentment there I'll realize,
as I hear the water skip.

I will sit for many hours there,
or at least what seems to be,
and I'll hear the water sing His care,
of the love He has for me.

And my troubles will go down the way,
where the ravens tend to flock,
yet the perfect peace of God will stay,
trusting well on Peaceful Rock.

Come unto me, all ye that labour
and are heavy laden, and I will give you rest.
Matthew 11:28

O taste and see that the LORD is good:
blessed is the man that trusteth in him.
Psalm 34:8

Blackberries

For Matthew

Blackberries ripen, full and sweet,
to make for me an August treat.
Their goodness calls me, "Come and dine!",
so up I climb to make them mine.

Safe underneath the ash and beech,
the berries grow within my reach.
I pluck them quickly for my pail
and eat my fill along the trail.

Blackberries splendid, good and free,
are like the graces given me.
God's fruit is for the picking ones,
and with it, love and mercy comes.

And David and all the house of Israel
played before the LORD on all manner
of instruments made of fir wood, even
on harps, and on psalteries, and on timbrels,
and on cornets, and on cymbals.
2 Samuel 6:5

August Sonnet

Raise voices like the singing crickets make
in August, when they start to stridulate.
In summer heat, and for our season's sake,
match all the buzz cicadas resonate.
Crash cymbals through dark troubles quick and sharp.
With louder tymbals, drum out jubilee.
Beat sistrums with the angel's ringing harp,
and tap a tune with Heaven's tympani.
But, I know every tiny abdomen
will, one day, be a chamber passed away.
Yet, for my merry soul, a glad 'amen'
sings out the promise of eternal's day.
So long as Christ lets voices amplify.
So long as hearts are raised to glorify.

There is a way which seemeth right unto a man,
but the end thereof are the ways of death.
Proverbs 14:12

Forest Winds

The September winds are kicking up,
  and the poplars, all so grandy,
  along the road are saying, "Turn!
  Your way is not too dandy!"

Their silvery leaves are showing me,
  as the sun falls in, and merry,
  that the way I go is not that good,
  and I'd best let someone carry—

Carry me to where the birches dance,
  and the ferns, on a wind a-borning,
  do swirl and twirl, as I listen well,
  to their end-of-summer warning—

Warning of the way that I think's right,
  which is not, to be contrary,
  for there are commandments to obey,
  and they're anything but airy!

Autumn

So shall my word be that
goeth forth out of my mouth:
it shall not return unto to me void,
but it shall accomplish that which I please,
and it shall prosper in the thing whereto I sent it.
For ye shall go out with joy, and be led forth with peace:
the mountains and the hills shall break forth before you
into singing, and all the trees of the field shall clap their hands.
Isaiah 55:11-12

The Trees of the Field

The colors of life are in the fall
where God's bright truths are shown to all.
The trees of the field will clap their hands
and spread God's love throughout the lands.

The warmest brown leaves tell it straight,
"All have sinned and tend to hate."
Red shiny leaves sing of love
that comes from God who reigns above.

Brightest orange leaves make all see:
"Christ bore all iniquity."
And pure yellow leaves give a smile
to be with Him in just a while.

The colors of fall are rich to see
the Painter of Eternity.
The trees of the field, forever true,
display God's love for me and you.

The Fruit of the Tree

It's Autumn and the harvest time
when the apple trees are bearing
sweet fruit that's worth a mile-long hike
and the afternoon for sharing.

We will know the apple trees we seek
by the goodness they are yielding,
by the bounty they have rich in store,
and the fragrance all so pleasing.

But the trees that have no tasty fruit
and are pleasant not for eyeing,
offer branches that are mostly bare,
and some look as though they're dying!

In the rosy light, we'll choose the best,
and our baskets we'll be filling;
the love of Jesus in our hearts
will, with grace, be over-spilling!

But the fruit of the Spirit is
love, joy, peace, longsuffering,
gentleness, goodness, faith, meekness,
temperance: against such there is no law.
Galatians 5;22-23

Jesus saith unto him,
I am the way, the truth, and the life:
no man cometh unto the Father, but by me.
John 14:6

The Orange Leaf
For Ezra

Gorgeously brilliant, a true, bright hue,
a one-of-a-kind, a marvelous view.
And there I see it beam in the sun,
the perfect orange leaf unlike any one.

Ongoing giver, the star of spring,
a dainty orange tree, a new life to bring.
And there I trace it, sent through the sky,
the free swirling seed that came from up high.

Delicate showcase, the crown of fall,
an emblem of change, the best of them all.
And there I catch it, crisp in the air,
the Maple Tree's Gift that none can compare!

Flying Leaves

Shall we not trust with grateful heart
the Maker of our Autumn's start,
who sends a briskly, whirlwind breeze
to cast off readied treetop leaves?
A gust! A flight!
The wind is right—
for flying leaves.

Shall we not see, on winds born high,
the sending forth of days gone by,
like when a flock of geese fly o'er,
or eagles climb up even more?
They turn! They fly!
Into the sky—
to soar on more.

Shall we not all together sing
the anthem of our gracious King,
who gives the old a lasting new
and answers longings faithful, true?
We go! We know!
The promised show—
in voices true.

The LORD hath appeared of old unto me,
saying, Yea, I have loved thee
with an everlasting love:
therefore with lovingkindness
have I drawn thee.
Jeremiah 31:3

Frost in Veery Glade

Autumn Sonnet

Pain is a time, like frost in Veery Glade,
when coated iced-dead leaves plink-plank the ground.
Remember Mary's tears in sorrows made?
Remember Stephen's wounds in brutal sound?
Within these woods, I see a misty breath
that weaves between the trees of darker space.
In troubled days of life and passing death,
I feel the coldness sharply on my face.
And damage to the heart from times of loss
is what my Savior must already know.
The hurting, bitter season of the cross
gives tears and wounds a reason, white as snow.
So by this pain, I call to Him who made
the falling leaves from frost in Veery Glade.

But I say unto you, Love your enemies,
bless them that curse you, do good to them that hate you,
and pray for them which despitefully use you, and persecute you;
that ye may be the children of your Father which is in heaven:
for he maketh his sun to rise on the evil and on the good,
and sendeth rain on the just and on the unjust.
Matthew 5:44-45

And he spake a parable unto them
to this end, that men ought always
to pray, and not to faint.
Luke 18:1

A Forest Night

The leaves have fallen from the trees,
save the willowy group of tamaracks;
and the coyotes yip in the rustling leaves
with the moonlight on their backs.

The shadows grow in the chilly air
and the wind brings out an owl,
and they know that winter will bring its share
when the coyotes start to howl.

Yet, they hold on fast through the stirring night,
like the ones who always pray,
having faith and trust in the morning light
and hope for a brand new day.

By him therefore let us offer the sacrifice of praise
To God continually, that is, the fruit of our lips
Giving thanks to his name.
Hebrews 13:15

Woodland Praise

It is high noon and the sunshine pours
on the pine trees standing stately,
raising gateways and old ancient doors
as the woodland sings whom it adores--
everlasting praises greatly.

In the grove, there is magnificence,
the most highest name exalting;
glory, admiration, one can sense,
even stones cry out the difference--
everlasting King extolling.

On the frost beneath my grateful feet,
in cathedrals, high and lofty,
I thank my Savior there I meet,
who sits upon the right hand seat--
everlasting love graciously.

In stalwart groves, by icy streams,
through creation that is honoring,
magnifying Christ who rightly deems,
from the woodlands to the sea that teems--
everlasting kingdom revering.

Winter

If we live in the Spirit,
let us also walk in the Spirit.
Galatians 5:25

Tracks in the Snow

A glistening dell,
white-clad and temple-like,
a line of fresh-made tracks
beneath a spruce's spike,
where winds have not come in
to shake the boughs of snow,
and in a winter's blue,
the sunlight shimmers low.

It's here we see a pattern,
while breathing crisp air,
the prints of whitetail deer
preserved in snowy care.
The pointed toes had followed
the ones before them made,
and dainty ones, too,
had crossed the frozen glade.

The wisest and the learned
trust in established ways
through cold and drifted trials
to kinder, warmer days;
So, let us raise a prayer
and speak our human need—
to walk within the footsteps
of Sovereign-made lead.

Chickadees

A Winter Sonnet

When to the mornings of uneasy thought,
I weigh the burden of a troubled heart,
and loathe the wayward steps I thought to plot
in harbored hurt before love had a start.
Then, sink I will to bearing no ill will,
if, through the day, I let the hatred win,
and find the snares kill hope to lift and thrill
the promise coming from my Maker's Kin.
And, far from marvels resting in a tree,
and long from simple calls of merriment,
and gone from basking in a guarantee,
my way would fail in winter's harshness spent.
But, if the while I think on chickadees,
a prayer can grow love for such as these.

Rejoiceth not in iniquity, but rejoiceth in the truth;
beareth all things, believeth all things,
hopeth all things, endureth all things.
1 Corinthians 13:6-7

But thou, Bethlehem Ephratah, though thou be little
among the thousands of Judah, yet out of thee
shall he come forth unto me that is to be ruler in Israel;
whose goings forth have been from of old, from everlasting.
Micah 5:2

The Sapling's Star

The night is cold, it is bitter cold,
and the trees are moving, creaking,
screeching in the cold, dark, winter night,
as the stars begin their peeking.

They can see the patch where the maples grow,
nestled in for winter, napping,
and beneath the trunk of a mighty red,
they can see the smallest sapling.

They are shown a strength in its tiny limbs,
of a promise building, keeping,
of a hope to give unsparingly,
of love for the woodland sleeping.

And they wonder who is showing this,
in whose light a-basking, savoring?
High above the sapling is its Star,
shining brightly, ever favoring!

Boughs of Hemlock

Boughs of hemlock, full, adorning,
blessed to greet the chilly morning;
as when Magi came afar,
from the east, beneath the Star,
and gave their gifts to the King of kings,
Creator of created things,
who became a man—a babe to carry—
and trusted the goodness of Joseph and Mary.

Boughs of hemlock, rich and stately,
by the roadside waving greatly;
likened to the branches' way
in Jerusalem that day,
when our Savior Jesus wept,
and on the road to the cross, kept,
to atone for us eternal peace
from sin's sure hold— a sure release.

Boughs of hemlock, sprinkled snow,
delicate grace on branches show;
like the change from winter time to spring.
A new life planted, faith will bring
fruit and life from a spirit clean,
and the harvest of an evergreen.
Trust and honor in scripture well
will be honored, as time will tell.

And ye shall take you on the first day
the boughs of goodly trees, branches of palm trees,
and the boughs of thick trees, and willows of the brook;
and ye shall rejoice before the LORD your God seven days.
Leviticus 23:40

For unto you is born this day in the city of David
a Saviour, which is Christ the Lord.
And this shall be a sign unto you;
Ye shall find the babe wrapped in swaddling clothes,
lying in a manger.
Luke 2:11-12

Joy in the Hollow

Joy, that blissful state to keep,
is met in a winter hollow,
where tracks lead in, both wide and deep,
by the edge of the firs on landscape steep,
and where I, with wonder, follow.

Over head, the sun is perfect light
on the snowy altered tree,
and the downy bridesmaid's hearty flight
is joined by grouse in peaceful sight,
where the woods are hushed for me.

You, Maker of my spirit's smile
by the marriage you impart,
declare a goodness for my while.
With a skip, I'll go another mile,
having joy within my heart.

Trust in the LORD with all thine heart;
and lean not unto thine own understanding.
In all thy ways acknowledge him,
and he shall direct thy paths.
Proverbs 3:5-6

THE iCY, GNARLY ELM

The icy, gnarly elm alone
in the dell, just beyond the spruces,
has taken on to moan and groan
and wonder of her uses,
to worry in the winter scene
where none but harshness grows—
and the cold wind blows.

Yet even so, the elm stands firm,
though the weighted ice is building.
And there lies at core a diseasing worm
as the branches soon are breaking.
Forbidding is the winter scene
in which all things are made weak—
where the plight looks bleak.

But there is remembrance of who one is,
as the sun shines on and sparkles.
Even through the strain and brittleness,
there is reason yet for marvels.
Hostile may the winter scene become,
and the stressful toll long—
but her trust is strong.

But as many as received him, to them gave he
power to become the sons of God,
even to them that believe on his name.
John 1:12

Snow of the Evergreen

Jesus, Jehovah, Immanuel.
Abundant joy rich to tell.
There is a love that fills my heart,
like snow in the deepest part.

El, Creator, Merciful, Love.
Blessed assurance from above.
There is a peace from Heaven's crown,
like snow gently falling down.

Savior, Messiah, Adonai.
Blood outpoured to sanctify.
There is a grace from only Him,
like snow coating every limb.

Unspeakable Gift, Redeemer, King.
Sing the song the ransomed sing.
There is a life made wholly right,
like snow turning woodlands white.

Spirit, Counselor, Author, Friend.
Kingdom wonders never end.
There is a seal that is lasting, clean,
like snow on the evergreen.

Additional Selected Scripture

And out of the ground made the LORD God to grow every tree that is pleasant to the sight, and good for food; the tree of life also in the midst of the garden, and the tree of knowledge of good and evil. Genesis 2:9

Then shall the trees of the wood sing out at the presence of the LORD, because he cometh to judge the earth. 1 Chronicles 16:33

And he shall be like a tree planted by the rivers of water, that bringeth forth his fruit in his season; his leaf also shall not wither; and whatsoever he doeth shall prosper. Psalm 1:3

And there shall come forth a rod out of the stem of Jesse, and a Branch shall grow out of his roots. Isaiah 11:1

A good tree cannot bring forth evil fruit, neither can a corrupt tree bring forth good fruit. Matthew 7:18

On the next day much people that were come to the feast, when they heard that Jesus was coming to Jerusalem, took branches of palm trees, and went forth to meet him, and cried, Hosanna: Blessed is the King of Israel that cometh in the name of the Lord. John 12:12-13

Christ hath redeemed us from the curse of the law, being made a curse for us: for it is written, Cursed is every one that hangeth on a tree. Galatians 3:13

Blessed are they that do his commandments, that they may have right to the tree of life, and may enter in through the gates into the city. Revelation 22:14

Dear Reader,

Seasons of Love: Woodland Poems of God's Love
was originally written and illustrated
to celebrate the fifty years God gave me.
The poems are based on real trees and places
around our home in Truxton, New York.
I hope you know that God loves us exceedingly!
May you enjoy the Lord's very best!
And, one day, may we walk together
in the woods of Heaven.

Here is another book that might encourage you:

Unto Us: A Christmas Poetry Book
was written and illustrated to celebrate
the birth of our Savior. Each poem and illustration
highlights a person, past and present, in the
amazing true events of God's lovely gift to us
—the birth of His Son, Jesus Christ.
Take time to meditate on the
true meaning of Christmas.

More information about my
books can be found at:
poemsandprayer.blogspot.com.
Thank you for your support.

Remember to keep praying.
God bless you as you trust Him!
Lisa

Made in the USA
Middletown, DE
29 September 2023

38940735R00042